Spring Cleaning For Heart and Home
A prayerful journey to a clean home

By Amy Terry
Free resources to compliment this study
at

www.RefocusedBibleStudy.com

Spring has sprung, and not only are there bunnies hopping around in the green grass, there are dust bunnies on my furniture. The animals are popping their heads back up from their underground burrows and living life again, but the piles of stuff under the beds in my house haven't seen the light of day since long before winter started. My heart sinks when I think about all that needs to get done in my house. It's time for a

~~Spring Cleaning!~~

But why spend so many hours mindlessly going through our houses when we can pray scripture that will bring a powerful cleansing of our Spirit and our family's spirits as we bag up, scrub, and shine our way to a clean house and clean hearts!

For the next four weeks, we will push our sleeves up, hit our knees, pray, scrub, and praise the God who has given us these temporary dwellings to live the most precious moments of this life in. Why only clean when we can consecrate? Why simply scrub when we can sanctify? Let's ask Jesus to come through our homes with us, and call on him to cleanse our hearts as we spray and wipe the dirt away.

~~Let's Bring Holy into Housework~~

We will focus on one area a week:

Week 1~~Drawers and Closets
Week 2 ~~Master Bedroom, lights, entryway
Week 3~~Kids Bedrooms, doors
Week 4~~Kitchen, Living Areas

You will need at least 30 minutes a day, 15 for time in this workbook, and 15 for sleeves rolled up work! Or your may choose to do all your cleaning on the weekends; see the weekly cleaning schedule in back of the study.

The goal of this study is to:
*Gain divine inspiration for spring cleaning from God's Word.
*Focus on one verse a day as you clean an area in your house.
*Learn to pray while you are cleaning.
*Make a habit of holy housework.

So let's get started with this invitation to set to work with Jesus on making our homes sparkle. May he be our constant reason and companion!

"Walk with me and work with me—watch how I do it. Learn the unforced rhythms of grace. I won't lay anything heavy or ill-fitting on you. Keep company with me and you'll learn to live freely and lightly." Matthew 11:29-30 MSG

As we embark on this journey, let it be our purpose to walk with Jesus through our homes, to live more freely and lightly when we are completed with this mission than when we started. Instead of being overwhelmed with the amount of work that needs to be done, let us do exactly what Jesus tells us to do in the passage above. Let's walk with him through our homes, being thankful for what he has given us. Working with him to minimize. Working with him to clear out so we don't have a heavy and ill-fitting amount of unnecessary stuff to manage. Keeping company with him the whole time, asking his blessing over the rooms we are working in, and the precious people we hold so dear who inhabit them. He is faithful to help us live more freely and lightly with him. Stop and pray now, committing to walk on this journey with Him. On the next page, write a prayer based on this passage, committing and inviting Jesus to be your companion on this journey to lightness and freedom in your home.

~Week 1~
~~Day 1~~
Drawers and Closets
Proverbs 31

20 She extends a helping hand to the poor
and opens her arms to the needy.
21 She has no fear of winter for her household,
for everyone has warm clothes.
22 She makes her own bedspreads.
She dresses in fine linen and purple gowns.
23 Her husband is well known at the city gates,
where he sits with the other civic leaders.
24 She makes belted linen garments
and sashes to sell to the merchants.
25 She is clothed with strength and dignity,
and she laughs without fear of the future.

It's a good thing we asked Jesus to walk with us and help us on this journey, because I am tired and overwhelmed after reading the passage above! If I tried to do all of those things in my own strength, I would give up before the first load of clothes needed to go to the dryer! Let's just focus on one verse a day and let Jesus have his way in our hearts with it, using it to fuel us and empower us to work a little each day.

Verse of the day: *"She extends a helping hand to the poor and opens her arms to the needy."*
Proverbs 31:20

We have the perfect opportunity to spread the love of Jesus through passing on some of the excess of clothes in our homes to a people in need. To us, they may seem out of date or old. But to someone who needs them, they can serve as a reminder that they are loved by their provider in heaven. Reaching out to those in need around us, as this verse states can be as simple as taking a bag of our cleaned out drawers to them. On the next page, thank God for the overflowing amount of clothes you have. Then ask him to direct you to who will be blessed and drawn closer to him by receiving some of the excess.

_____

_____

_____

_____

_____

_____

_____

_____

_____

_____

_____

Now let's get to work! Grab a trash bag and set to work clearing one of the areas of clothing in your house, where you start is up to you. Just get going, thanking God for providing the clothes for you and now for someone else. Set a timer for at least 15 minutes to stay focused, or commit to doing it at a certain time this week or weekend.

~Week 1~
~~Day 2~~
Drawers and Closets

Verse of the Day: *"She has no fear of winter for her household, for everyone has warm clothes." Proverbs 31:21*

Winter is over! I don't know about you, but I am so happy to write those three words. I am ready for flip-flops and sunshine. The principle the Proverbs 31 woman displays in the verse above is that she is ready for the change of the seasons. We certainly aren't going to send our kids out to play in the weeks to come in their snow boots. So let's decide what to do with the winter clothes and let us prepare for the change of the seasons.

Today, go through your children's clothes for the change of the seasons. Thank God for the precious memories he showered your family with as you put away or bag up to give away the clothes they wore in this past winter. Children are one of the sweetest gifts from the Lord. Make this a special time between you and him, praising him for your most precious gifts, your children. Thank him that they are healthy and

growing out of their clothes.
Keep a list below of clothing items they need for the spring and summer:

_____

_____

_____

_____

_____

_____

_____

_____

_____

_____

_____

~Week 1~
~~Day 3~~
Drawers and Closets

Verse of the Day: *"She makes her own bedspreads and she dresses in fine linen and purple gowns."*
Proverbs 31:22

For me, this verse means "She goes to Target and buys a new bedspread, and she gets a new dress while she's there. Can I get an amen, sister? If you enjoy sewing you don't have to amen to that, keep on threading, girl.

For this day of reflection and work, I am going to be going through my linen closets. I feel bad for my husband when he opens them up. I think he is scared he is going to be the victim of a sheet avalanche if he turns the knob to grab a towel.

I have a few odd closets in my house that store things like board games and old pictures, and I am going to go through them today. Let's clear out and make room to live freely and lightly.

As we move into these drawers and closets

today, let's pattern our prayers to clear out the clutter in our hearts as well. Let an avalanche of the hidden concerns deep within your soul that you never get around to voicing to God come out today. As you de-junk physically, let Jesus clear out the junk that is making your heart heavy and overwhelmed.

As you see the closet or drawers you work in today become clean and organized, I pray your spirit soars with lightness as you let every concern in your soul be lifted up, out and into the hands of your heavenly father. You aren't supposed to hold on to them, anymore than you are supposed to hold onto all of this needless stuff you are bagging up today. GET RID OF IT!

Below, make a list of things you will be praying about as you clean out clutter today:

_____

_____

_____

_____

_____

~Week 1~
~~Day 4~~
Drawers and Closets

Verse of the Day: *"Her husband is well known at the city gates, where he sits with the other civic leaders." Proverbs 31:23*

Today we are focusing in on blessing our husbands. This will look different for each of us. I would suggest asking them before you go cleaning out their drawers and closet for them! The underlying theme in the verse above that we want to put into action today is that we want our man to feel respected at home. If he feels respected at home, he will feel worthy of respect outside of the home, where he is "sitting and serving," (at his job, in the community, in church, etc.).

Where is the area of clutter we need to dejunk for them? I will be going through my husband's drawers and closet. Wherever it is, today is about blessing him through cleaning out stuff and lifting him up in prayer. If you aren't in a good place in your marriage right now, then stop and pray, asking God to clear your heart out first. Pour out your heart to Jesus before you set your hands to work. Jesus is always concerned with the heart of the matter, so let's start there.

Wherever your heart is in your marriage, ask God to make it into a sacrificial servant today, blessing your husband through this work. Enter into today's work with no expectations of applause from anyone but Jesus. It is a gift to your husband.

List below what is in your heart to pray over your husband as you clear out "stuff" for him today. Stay focused in prayer for him the entire time you clean today.

_____

_____

_____

_____

_____

_____

_____

~Week 1~
~~Day 5~~
Drawers and Closets

Verse of the Day: *"She is clothed with strength and dignity, and she laughs without fear of the future." Proverbs 31:25*

I pray that prayerfully cleaning out your drawers and closets this week has left you feeling strong and dignified, free and light, so that you can laugh without fear of opening them up!

In the verse above, the strength and dignity of the Proverbs 31 woman is found in Jesus alone. She doesn't' find it in the order and cleanliness of her drawers and closets. She doesn't laugh without fear for the future because she has her spring and summer wardrobe shopping list prepared and the money set aside to buy what is needed. She laughs and lives freely and lightly because she trusts in Jesus to give her strength to serve her family and to provide all their needs.

Today we are going pull the pride out of the drawers and closets of our hearts. Let's ask Jesus to take out the reasons for homemaking that are less than loving him and loving our families. Let's ask him to remove the lies that we can't do the things he has asked us to do.

Let's take off the clothes that we have been wearing and put on the strength and dignity that come from walking and working with Jesus in our homes. Use the space below to ask him to help you maintain the spaces you have cleared out together, and to follow through with what still needs to be done in drawers and closets in your home. Use today and this weekend to finish the work!

~Week 2~
~~Day 1~~
Master Bedroom
Song of Songs 2

8 Ah, I hear my lover coming!
He is leaping over the mountains,
bounding over the hills.
9 My lover is like a swift gazelle
or a young stag.
Look, there he is behind the wall,
looking through the window,
peering into the room.
10 My lover said to me,
"Rise up, my darling!
Come away with me, my fair one!
11 Look, the winter is past,
and the rains are over and gone.
12 The flowers are springing up,
the season of singing birds has come,
and the cooing of turtledoves fills the air.
13 The fig trees are forming young fruit,
and the fragrant grapevines are blossoming.
Rise up, my darling!
Come away with me, my fair one!

Translation of this passage for me: Oh no! I have to hurry and get around to cleaning the bedroom, he just called and he has boarded the flight to come home! I quickly tidy up what I can before my husband gets home so I can at least attempt to make our bedroom a place of refuge and rest away from the rest of the house.

I love Song of Solomon, because it paints a beautiful picture for marriage. It is a metaphor of how Christ loves his bride, the church, but it also gives us married couples a beautiful look at the passion this sacred relationship was meant to hold.

Verse of the Day: *"Ah, I hear my lover coming! He is leaping over the mountains, bounding over the hills.." Song of Songs 2:8*

The woman in the scripture *heard* her lover coming and prepared for his arrival. God created men with a need to be heard and respected. "So again I say, each man must love his wife as he loves himself, and the wife must respect her husband, "Ephesians 5:33.

Have you heard your husband say anything specific lately that needs to be done in the bedroom (cleaning wise, ladies :)! If so, make this the first thing on your list this week. If you

haven't, then start with the bed itself.
___ Dust the headboard.
___Check the condition of your sheets and pillows
___ Clean out under your bed.

All the while as you clean, pray for your marriage. Below are some scriptures to pray today, and you can continue to pray these over your marriage everyday when you make your bed. Post them if you need to. Work on memorizing them so you can pray them anytime over your marriage.

"I pray _____ will love me like Christ loved the church, and that he will daily lay his life down for me like Christ did." Ephesians 5:25

"I pray you will help me to submit to _____ out of reverence for you, and to respect him." Ephesians 5:24, 33.

"I pray that we will be united as one." Ephesians 5:31.

~Week 2~
~~Day 2~~
Master Bedroom

Verse of the Day: *"My lover is like a swift gazelle or a young stag. Look, there he is behind the wall, looking through the window, peering into the room." Song of Songs 2:9*

The reality is that this room that is supposed to be a "lover's getaway' is also a room that is lived in. And if your husband is looking very closely at the walls or peering through the windows, he may be seeing some dirt built up from that real living.

As we wash the walls and windows of our bedroom, lets pray with focus on what we allow to come into our marriage, and set up protective walls around our marriage to keep it safe from the world.

Psalm 91 is a "go to" chapter as a prayer for protection. If you have time, read it, thinking about your marriage and praying over its protection. Pray for God to protect your marriage from any person or thing that would harm it.

Write down your favorite verse from the chapter referring to protection of your marriage below and write out what you will be praying specifically to our God on high who protects your marriage!

_____
_____
_____
_____
_____
_____
_____
_____
_____
_____
_____
_____

Now get to cleaning those walls and windows, or commit to a time this week to do so.

~Week 2~
~~Day 3~~
Master Bedroom and Lights

Verse of the Day: *"My lover said to me, "Rise up, my darling! Come away with me, my fair one!" Song of Songs 2:10*

Today we are going to be focusing on the two things we do when we rise in the morning: Turn on the light and go to the bathroom. It's funny, I know! We are going to start by dusting the light fixture in our bedroom while we pray this scripture over our marriage:

Write out John 1:4 below:

_____

_____

_____

As you clean the light fixtures in your master bedroom and bathroom today, pray that Jesus himself will shine the light of life on your marriage. Pray that his light will penetrate and bring new life to any places that feel dark or dead in your relationship. As followers of Christ, we have the light of the world living in us. The closer we walk with Jesus, the brighter his light shines through us. Take a few minutes below, asking Jesus to draw you and everyone in your family closer to him, so that you all can be vessels of his light shining through you.

> *"You are the light of the world--like a city on a hilltop that cannot be hidden."* Matthew 5:14

_____

_____

_____

_____

_____

_____

_____

Now go clean the light fixtures through the rest of the house, along with the light switch panels, I know they need a scrubbing here!

~Week 2~
~~Day 4~~
Master Bedroom and Bathrooms

Now let's make the bathrooms sparkle!
Below is a checklist of tasks to accomplish while you pray these specific verses:

___Mirror: Pray we can be full of God's Spirit so that "we can be **mirrors that brightly reflect** the glory of the Lord," 2 Corinthians 3:18

___ Toilet: Pray you will **rid yourself** of any "anger rage, malicious behavior, slander, and dirty language," Colossians 3:8

___Tub/Shower: Pray 2 Corinthians 7:1, "Because we have these promises, dear friends, let us **cleanse ourselves** from everything that can defile our body or spirit. And let us work toward complete holiness because we fear God."

Before setting to work, reflect on the next page how Jesus would have you apply them to your life at the present time. Also write down ways you can pray for your family members in light of these verses, not to judge them, but to pray over their weaknesses, to strengthen them in Christ

~Week 2~
~~Day 5~~
Entryway

Verse of the Day: *"The flowers are springing up, the season of singing birds has come and the cooing of turtledoves fills the air... Raise up, my darling! Come away with me, my fair one!" Song of Songs 2:12-13*

"Let the wife make the husband glad to come home, and let him make her sorry to see him leave." ~Martin Luther

To finish off the week, let's work on the entryway of our home, inside and outside. We want our home to be inviting in everyway, most of all for our husband and children, but also for anyone who enters it.

With spring comes the promise of new life in Christ. Let's sweep away the dust, shine the door, and consider a new welcome mat and spring flowers!

Read and reflect on the verse below, then write out a prayer asking Jesus to be the most welcome and real person in your marriage, family, and home.

"Look! I stand at the door and knock. If you hear my voice and open the door, I will come in, and we will share a meal together as friends."
Revelation 3:20

~Week 3~
~~Day 1~~
Kids' Bedrooms

Psalm 127

"**1** Unless the LORD builds a house,
the work of the builders is wasted.
Unless the LORD protects a city,
guarding it with sentries will do no good.
2 It is useless for you to work so hard
from early morning until late at night,
anxiously working for food to eat;
for God gives rest to his loved ones.
3 Children are a gift from the LORD;
they are a reward from him.
4 Children born to a young man
are like arrows in a warrior's hands.
5 How joyful is the man whose quiver is full of them! He will not be put to shame when he confronts his accusers at the city gates.

Remember when you were preparing the nursery for the child inside your womb whose face you had yet to see? Everything was going to be perfect. Every valuable, useable thing was going to have a perfect place, to be used and then put back perfectly. You spent hours rocking your sweet babies in this sanctuary set aside for the most precious moments of motherhood.

Then things got crazy. The baby cried real loud and you decided to toss the sleeper on the floor instead of in the perfectly placed hamper, three feet away. And your perfect plan for a perfectly kept child's room never regained its perfection. Instead, it became a sacred place of real living; of laughter and dance parties, of dress up shows when you throw clothes all over the place, of inside ball games and tickle mania. Your perfect plan took a turn, and turned out even better.

The only problem is, we can't find any clean socks. So let's enter with caution so we don't trip on anything, and invite Jesus into this space. Let's make this spring cleaning a holy one, that lathers the grace of God over our children and over the place they rest their heads.

Verse of the Day: *"Unless the LORD builds a house, the work of the builders is wasted. Unless the LORD protects a city, guarding it with sentries will do no good."*
Psalm 127:1

Even with all the diligence we put into protecting our babies, they have all gotten hurt in this dangerous, fallen world we walk in. Scrapped knees and wounded hearts happen. Thankfully, there is an all powerful, all knowing, all seeing God whom we can call upon to protect them.

On the next page, write out a prayer of protection over your children. Reflect on the verse above and let it be the starting point of your prayer. When time allows, scrub the walls in your child's room, and as you do, pray the Lord's protection over them the entire time. Some areas to remember to ask the Lord to protect in their lives include: their relationship with Him, their future spouse, their sexual purity, their physical protection, their identity and self esteem. These are just starting points. Let the Spirit of God guide your prayers of protection for them.

~Week 3~
~~Day 2~~
Kids' Bedrooms

Verse of the Day: *"It is useless for you to work so hard from early morning until late at night, anxiously working for food to eat;"* Psalm 127:2a

"Play is the work of the child." -Maria Montessori

I've been to places in the world where baby dolls are made out of old plastic bottles and toy cars are bended pieces of scrap metal. Children will play with what they have available. If you are reading this, then you probably have an abundance of toys for your children to play with.

Who am I kidding? When our toy boxes need a clear out at my house, it is usually because the kids have quit playing because we have so much, they can't find anything!

Childhood play is such a gift from the Lord, because we know what is coming for our children. The older they become, the more responsibility they will have. The weight of the world is rushing in earlier than ever in the lives of our children. Soon the truth God warns us of in the verse of the day will threaten to steal joy from their lives. So let them play!

Ask the Lord to bless your child's playtime. Ask him to remind you of how important it is to spend time playing with your children. Lately, I have tried to make sure I play at least 15 minutes with each of my children everyday. Make this a priority. Playtime with your children is a time you will never look back and regret. Pray it will show your children a glimpse of how their heavenly father wants to be involved in every part of their lives, just like you do. Pray for the Lord to give you words to convey his truth and love during moments of play together.

When time allows, go through your children's toys. This is a great opportunity for you to teach your child the generosity of Christ. Encourage them to be involved in bagging up toys and taking them to a friend or a donation agency.

~Week 3~
~~Day 3~~
Kids' Bedrooms

Verse of the Day: *"for God gives rest to his loved ones." Psalm 127:2b*

Rest is a gift from the Lord. From the very first story in their baby storybook bibles, we read to our children about the seventh day, when God rested. He didn't rest because he was tired, for God never grows weak or weary (Isaiah 40:28). He rested to show us a cycle of work and rest that helps us retreat, refuel, and become re-energized.

Today we will be praying over our children's rest in the Lord. As you clean up around their bed, under their bed, their headboard, and the area around it, pray the verses below. You may also want to teach them to your children if they are old enough to make their own beds, so that they can pray them as well.

Turn the following scriptures into prayers for your children on the spaces on the next page.

"Come to me, all you who are weary and burdened, and I will give you rest." Matthew 11:28

"In peace I will lie down and sleep, for you alone, LORD, make me dwell in safety." Psalm 4:8

"He makes me lie down in green pastures, he leads me beside quiet waters, he refreshes my soul." Psalm 23:2-3

~Week 3~
~~Day 4~~
Kids' Bedrooms

Verses of the day: "3 Children are a gift from the LORD; they are a reward from him. 4 Children born to a young man are like arrows in a warrior's hands." Psalm 127:3-4

Sometimes in the midst of messes, chaos, loudness, and stressors of mothering, we loose sight of the truth that our children are a treasure from the Lord. Little seeds of grumbling and complaining enter into our hearts because of the never ending work that being a mom entails. One of the greatest methods of defense against this is to remember what the bible says about our children and our high calling as mothers.

When we recall and think upon this truth to combat the grumpiness that all the hard work of motherhood brings, then our hearts and lips go from ungrateful to praiseful. Let's pull out and focus on this truth through the verses on the next page.

Answer the questions below concerning the two verses above. What does verse 3 say children are:

_____

_____

How does verse 4 describe the gift of children?

_____

_____

Turn these verses into a thankful prayer back to the Lord as you focus on shining up- the furniture in your child's room. Go through the book cases, dressers, desks, and any other furniture and dust, and shine it.

Also, pray over your child's bravery and discipline in growing in their knowledge of the Lord and following him, becoming a mighty warrior in the army of God.

While cleaning bookcases and desks pray:
"I pray that (child's name) _____'s love will overflow more and more, and that _____ will keep on growing in knowledge and understanding." Philippians 1:9

While cleaning your child's dresser, pray that he/she will daily put on the armor of God to protect them, from Ephesians 6:13-17:

Lord, help _____ put on every piece of God's armor so he/she will be able to resist the enemy in the time of evil. Then after battle he/she will be standing firm. Help them to stand their ground, putting on:

-the belt of truth
-the body armor of God's righteousness
-shoes of the peace
-the shield of faith
-Salvation as their helmet
-Sword of the Spirit, which is the Word of God

Pray these passages over your children in faith that our faithful Lord is listening, and acting on your children's behalf to do what you are asking!

~Week 3~
~~Day 5~~
Kids' Bedrooms

Verse of the Day: *"How joyful is the man whose quiver is full of them! He will not be put to shame when he confronts his accusers at the city gates." Psalm 127:5*

Yesterday we reclaimed our joy in motherhood as we reflected on what a gift from the Lord they are to us! We also prayed the armor of God over them as they fight the good fight beside us in this world.

Let's look at the context of verse 5. In the culture when this passage was written, having many children was considered a great blessing of the Lord. When there was a conflict between two men, they would meet at the city gates for judgment, and bring their sons to vouch for their character, and also to battle with them physically against their adversary.

Our children will no doubt be involved in conflicts in their lives, both with people and spiritually against the enemy. Pray over these conflicts as you scrub the "gate" of their room, their door, and door frame. Pray they will walk with integrity through these conflicts, and therefore, will not be put to shame.

There is another place in scripture where doorposts and gates are mentioned. It is in the book of Deuteronomy, chapter 6:

"Repeat them again and again to your children. Talk about them when you are at home and when you are on the road, when you are going to bed and when you are getting up. Tie them to your hands and wear them as reminders. **Write them on the doorposts of your house and on your gates."**

Here, Moses is commanding the people to live out the ten commandments. When Jesus walked on the earth, he said the whole law could be summed up as this in Matthew 22:37-40:

Jesus replied, "You must love the Lord your God with all your heart, all your soul, and all your mind. This is the first and greatest commandment. A second is equally important: "Love your neighbor as yourself. The entire law and all the demands of the prophets are based on these two commandments. "

Here we are reminded by Jesus of the most important thing for our children. Really, the only thing. To love the Lord and love others. Write out a prayer to the Lord below asking him to cultivate an incredible love for him in each of your children's hearts. Then continue to pray as you scrub their door, and every door in the house their sweet little messy hands have touched! Consider literally doing what Deuteronomy says and hanging a sign with the greatest commandment on it above one of the doors of your home.

~Week 4~
~~Day 1~~
Kitchen

Psalm 51

7 Purify me from my sins, and I will be clean; wash me, and I will be whiter than snow.

8 Oh, give me back my joy again; you have broken me- now let me rejoice.

9 Don't keep looking at my sins. Remove the stain of my guilt.

10 Create in me a clean heart, O God. Renew a loyal spirit within me.

11 Don not banish me from your presence, and don't take your Holy Spirit from me.

12 Restore to me the joy of your salvation, and make me willing to obey you.

The kitchen is considered the "heart" of a home. It is where people gather around to nourish their bodies, as well as their souls. It is where us mothers spend the majority of our time, as we prepare meals for the precious mouths the Lord has given us to serve. And boy, do they eat a lot! Am I right? It seems like just as soon as the kitchen is clean from the last meal, one of my growing little humans is walking towards the pantry!

I admit, sometimes the task of feeding my family seems overwhelming and that same complaining, grumbling attitude we discussed last week creeps back in. What a wasted opportunity to serve the Lord in gladness! It is like the food that has been in the back of the fridge too long. It was supposed to be satisfying, but instead, bacteria overtook it and ugly mold grew. Sin is like that bacteria. It festers and grows unless we confess it to the Lord and ask him to cleanse us.

Verse of the Day: *"Purify me from my sins, and I will be clean; wash me, and I will be whiter than snow." Psalm 51:7*

The King James Version of this verse uses the words, "Purge me with hyssop and I shall be clean, wash me, and I will be whiter than snow."

"To purge" makes me think of going through and tossing out all the old food that is not going to be used in my refrigerator and cabinets on a physical level. But let's not let this opportunity pass to purge our hearts as well while we do this Holy Housework. When time allows clean out and scrub your refrigerator and cabinets and their surfaces.

Ask the Lord's Spirit to guide you in this purging. Write out a prayer of confession below, but infuse it with the thankfulness of his cleansing. At the end of it, look at your sparkling white refrigerator interior and know your heart is white as snow as well, washed by the precious blood of Christ.

_____

_____

_____

_____

_____

_____

_____

~Week 4~
~~Day 2~~
Dining areas

Verse of the Day: *"Make me to hear joy and gladness; let the bones which you have broken rejoice." Psalm 51:8*

After" breaking our backs" in the kitchen, there is nothing like gathering with the people we love the most around the table and sharing a meal. Some of our best conversations and memories happen seated around our dinning tables. In fact, many studies have been done, showing that families who eat around their table together regularly have less conflict.

This is a great opportunity to pray over joy and gladness happening at our tables. The phrase "make me to hear" doesn't just mean audibly. It means spiritually, on a heart level. How often do we hear a whole lot of chattering and just ask the Lord to make it stop! Let's be honest, silent dinner sounds fun sometimes! But these are the little moments that we will look back on as the biggest moments.

The "bones which you have broken" refer to being broken by a consciousness of guilt like we studied yesterday, as we asked the Lord to purge all the sour things in our hearts that needed to be cleansed. Today, we REJOICE! The Lord has cleansed us and we feel like dancing as we scrub the tables we feast together at!

Below, turn the verse of the day into a prayer. Pray the Lord will help you making eating together as a family a priority, and pray for joy and gladness to be full at your tables. Pray not only for joy between your family members, but that together all of you will be glad in the Lord together, and that many of the conversations held at these tables will be about the Bread of Life, Jesus himself.

_____

_____

_____

_____

_____

_____

~Week 4~
~~Day 3~~
Living Areas

Verse of the Day: *"Don't keep looking at my sins. Remove the stain of my guilt."*
Psalm 51:9

How many times have you walked through the living areas of your house, seen something dirty, and thought, I've got to get around to cleaning that? Today is the day to quit looking at them, and remove them!

To "remove the sins of my guilt" literally means "to wipe away, or blot out" in its original Hebrew language. Take your bucket of soapy water and rag and go around your living room today, wiping away the dirt and grime from real living in your living room.

But first, reflect on the verse below, which will bring true freedom to you and all the people in your home. This verse reminds us of how the Lord does not continue to 'act upon" our past sins.

"He has removed our sins as far from us as the east is from the west." Psalm 103:12

How far has God removed your sin from you?

What an incredibly forgiving God we have! If only we had his spirit of forgiveness so quickly for our husbands and children! Below, right out a prayer asking God to help you be quick to completely forgive them when they disappoint you. Let the truth of how completely God forgives you make you quickly and completely forgive your loved ones.

~Week 4~
~~Day 4~~
Living Areas

Verse of the Day: *"Create in me a clean heart, O God. Renew a loyal spirit within me. Do not banish me from your presence, and don't take your Holy Spirit from me." Psalm 51:10-11*

Today we will center our focus around the couches and chairs where we sit around resting, being "renewed" and watching entertainment on the television. These days, it is so hard to sit around as a family and watch something that God would agree is clean. Let's write out a prayer below, asking God to transform the time our family relaxes on the couches. Ask him to make the bible and books be more frequently read than the TV turned on. Pray that when the TV is turned on, that it is something that is pleasing to him and clean to all of our blood bought hearts.

_____

_____

_____

_____

Now let's look at Psalm 51:10. What is David clearly asking God for?

_____

There is nothing like realizing you are in the presence of God. Psalm 16:11 says that in God's presence, there is fullness of joy. Don't you want a fullness of joy in your living room? Pray below that your family will have an ever increasing awareness of the presence of God in your entire home. Invite Jesus to be the most real and active member of your family. Let this prayer continue when you have time to clean the couches, chairs, and TV area in your home.

_____

_____

_____

~Week 4~
~~Day 5~~
Restoration

Verse of the Day: *"Restore to me the joy of your salvation, and make me willing to obey you." Psalm 51:12*

Today is our LAST spring cleaning study day! This is the perfect verse to end on, as we can look around, and feel a restoration in our homes, I pray we can feel it in our hearts as well!

The word "restore" in this verse means "to bring back, or refresh. Today is the day to kick your feet up, look around, and rest in the restoration inside you and around you. Today is the day to inhale the joy you have because you are a wife, mother, and homemaker who belongs to Jesus. You are not perfect at this. You never will be. Because people actually live in this house.

Write out a prayer on the next page asking the Lord to continually restore you to the joy in your salvation as you serve him in your home. Ask him to make housework holy to you, a spiritual act of worship.

_____

_____

_____

_____

Now, look towards the future of your holy housework. Ask the Lord to make your hands and habits strong. Ask him to help you obey him in the small things of caring for this temporary dwelling. Consider coming up with a weekly cleaning plan to help you.

"Commit your actions to the LORD, and your plans will succeed." Proverbs 16:3

_____

_____

_____

_____

_____

_____

_____

Cleaning Schedule

This is a weekly cleaning schedule that coincides with this study, for those who would like to clean on the weekends.

Week	Cleaning Tasks
Week 1	Closets Drawers
Week 2	Master bedroom Bed Windows Walls Lights Bathrooms Entryway of Home
Week 3	Kid's Bedrooms Walls Toys Beds Furniture All doors in house
Week 4	Kitchen Refrigerator Cabinets Living Room Walls Couch, chairs, TV

Made in the USA
Lexington, KY
11 April 2016